PROMISES TO MY PET

BY: CLAIRE CHEW, M.A. C.C.F.S

Promises To My Pet is a process that helps you think through and make a pledge about how you'll care for your pet throughout the duration of his life.

What is Promises To My Pet?

Promises To My Pet takes you through different scenarios and questions to help you formulate and record a plan to care for your animal friend from here on out. Promises To My Pet helps you to make healthcare decisions for your pet BEFORE they even begin to get sick--when you are not under emotional distress and can think clearly. This document serves as a record of your pet in his prime. The pain of losing a pet is often compounded by the fact that we have to be the one to decide when it's time to let our pet go. Promises To My Pet is a way for you to prepare for that time--before you face it.

How to use Promises To My Pet

Promises To My Pet is easy to use. This booklet is made up of sections that help you make an assessment of your pet's health. There are places to check a box, write a few sentences, and post photos, which will serve as visual reminders of their health. You can even choose to implement some of your decisions and plans right now, to ensure your animal's physical and emotional wellbeing. Include copies of your pet's identification. Sign it, along with a witness, and submit a copy to your veterinarian for your pet's files. You might even want to discuss this with your vet at your pet's next appointment to make sure you are both on the same page. You can review and add to this each year during your pet's routine check-up visit. Make copies for family members or pet sitters who may take care of your pet (and remember to consider the possibility of your pet outliving you).

Tip: Set aside plenty of time to think through these questions and fill this out. Don't rush it--take the time to do it right. Later, you will be glad you did.

How Promises To My Pet can help

It serves as a reminder of and helps you keep the promise you made the day you brought your pet home--the promise to love and care for him forever. Pets depend on us for all of their daily needs, and are a lifelong commitment. That means that we promise not to run our backs on our pets when the going gets tough--and sometimes, it can get really tough. Unforeseeable injuries or sickness (yours or theirs), life changes (like new jobs, homes, or family members), and financial limitations can make it challenging to care for a pet. That's why it is helpful to establish some written promises at several important stages of their life--starting now. A document like Promises To My Pet also allows for continuity in the care of your pet in the event that you are absent from home (temporarily or permanently), and they are left with a family member or a pet sitter.

Making a life or death decision about a sick pet is an emotional dilemma. Having a document of your promise to care for them can serve as an immensely helpful and comforting tool when we are faced with making one of life's most difficult decisions.

Why Promises To My Pet Was Created

I was inspired to create Promises To My Pet after seeing clients having to make life or death decisions about their beloved pets. Sometimes, the pet owners were not ready to say goodbye, and were plagued by guilt, wavering between having done too much or not enough. At other times, decisions came from a place of reacting emotionally to the information given and not having enough time to think it all the way through. I thought back to when I volunteered in a hospice some years ago, and became familiar with "Five Wishes" TM – an advance directive for humans, letting family and doctors know who they chose to make healthcare decisions for them when they can no longer do it themselves. It planted a seed. I thought, "what if pet owners had a similar guide for making healthcare decisions for their furry family members?"

I want pet parents to be left with the confidence that they did everything they could for their pet. Of course, it is natural to feel elements of blame, guilt, anger, or regret when it's time to say goodbye to our pets, but my mission with Promises to My Pet is to try to ease that a bit by giving us a tool to think through things before we need them so that when the time comes, we see ourselves through the lens of unconditional love. My hope is that, at the end of a pet's life, we can feel confident that we have done everything we can for our pet by following this plan. As a pet owner, this is the final gift you can give to your beloved furry family member (and yourself).

My Pet's Personal Details

Today's Date:

Pet's Name:

Pet's Date of Birth:

Species:

Breed:

Sex:

Color/Weight:

Pet cargiver's name:

Best Phone Number to contact in case of emergency:

Alternative contact:

The Basics- What Should Be In Your File

Below is a list of practical information that you should keep in a safe place in case of an emergency. With smart phones, there are many online apps that enable you to have digital records at your disposal wherever you go.

If you're missing any of these items, now is the time to find them. Be an ambassador for your pet's health and wellness with good record-keeping!

My Pet's Personal Details Please check off boxes when complete

- Proof of Ownership
- Adoption Papers
- Special Needs
- Certificates such as Rabies Shots, Inoculations, etc
- Pet License
- Microchip Information
- Emergency Contact Information
- Medical History (all in one place)
- Medication List

Below is a list of some of the things that may be included in the daily care of your pet. You probably already have this memorized in your head, but it is helpful to have lists written out and handy for your pet sitter or caregiver in your absence (planned or unplanned).

The Basics- What Should Be In Your File Please check off boxes when complete

- Daily Schedule
- Food/Feeding
- Supplies for Pet (including where they are kept)
- Exercise/Playtime
- Grooming
- Bedtime

Financial Care

Being a fiscally responsible owner is a big part of our commitment to our pets. Routine veterinary care is a huge part of keeping your pet happy and healthy! Whether you choose to go the traditional or holistic route, it can be helpful to create a budget for things such as check-ups and dental cleanings. Below is a list of items to consider.

Monthly Budget

Budget for food, treats, bedding, crate, leash, toys, and other general supplies

Budget for annual exams/wellness visits and alternative therapies

Budget for training or other behavior needs

Budget for unforeseen events (accidents or injuries)

Emergency fund for pre-arrangement authorization for services in case of an emergency

Emergency fund to create a living will or pet trust

When we plan a vacation, we think of the pet sitter, emergency contacts, and favorite toys, but sometimes, we overlook one of the most crucial things – giving your veterinary clinic, emergency clinic, or boarding facility the permission to pay for services in case of an emergency. You can obtain a "release of payment" form and fill it out prior to your trip.

Spend time thinking about your pet's long-term care. Who will take care of them in the event of your death? In many states, animals are still considered property and a human has to be in charge of them. How will your pet's care be paid for? One option is to a pet trust.

Refer to the ASPCA for more information (www.aspca.org).

PROMISE 1:

MY PROMISE TO CARE FOR YOU

PROMISE 1:

My Promise To Care For You

Please fill in the blanks and cross out anything that you disagree with.

On this date _______________________, I, _______________________, promise to give my pet,

_______________________, the best care possible, both physically and emotionally. I promise to carry
out the basic care listed below to the best of my ability.

I promise to feed my pet _______ times a day.

I promise to buy or make food that suits my pet's nutritional needs.

I promise to bath my pet at least _______ times per month.

I promise to brush my pet's coat _______times per month.

I promise to trim/check my pet's feet/nails.

I promise to groom/cut my pet's coat if needed.

I promise to brush my pet's teeth.

I promise to clean my pet's ears and eyes _______ times per month.

I promise to buy fun and engaging toys for my pet to play with.

I promise to play/walk with my pet _______ times per week.

I promise to pet-proof my home from dangerous materials (household cleansers,
chocolate, over-the-counter medications, etc)

I promise to pet-proof my yard from dangerous plants (lilies, etc), and make sure
it is secure so he doesn't escape.

I promise to always keep a collar with current ID tags on my pet.

PROMISE 2:

HOW I WANT TO BE REMEMBERED

PROMISE 2:

How I Want To Be Remembered

Our pets have different personalities, just as humans do. Some are outgoing and funny, while others are sweet and shy. It's important to remember this as your pet ages. Similar to humans, our pets' natural functions decline with age. This may include their memory, or their sense of sight and smell. Sometimes, even their personalities change. They may forget commands they once knew, or exhibit aggressive behavior towards another family member who they used to adore. Alternatively, your pet may display increasing anxiety and clinginess, or-- on the other end of the spectrum--become less interested in engaging socially.

Whatever the case may be, it's good to document any changes you see over the years. It is important to have these records for comparison when your pet's health declines. It will really help you make assessments and decisions.

There are many personalities to consider. Below are some fun ones to try on your furry friend for size. Feel free to come up with your own.

Party animal – lives life on the wild side.

Nervous Nelly – sometimes anxious and dependent.

Worker Bee – needs a job to feel useful.

Teacher's Pet – eager to please.

Class Clown – fun and likes to play.

Tasmanian Devil – very athletic with a lot of energy.

Napoleon – a large personality in a small body.

Introvert Angel – loving and independent at the same time.

Most Popular – life of the party and loves the attention.

Trusted Sidekick- always by your side.

Personal Pledge

On this date, __________________________, I, ___________________________,

promise to remember my pet, ___________________________, as being happy,

healthy, and full of life. I promise to refer to my pet's quality of life when making

medical decisions on their behalf.

PROMISE 2 ACTIVITY:

I believe every life is precious and should be treated with dignity. When the time comes that our pets are very sick and cannot speak for themselves, it is helpful to have their wishes remembered as if they were in perfect health. Take a look at what you've documented above and then proceed to the section below.

The next two wishes deal with your pet's personal and emotional wishes. Our pets do not speak our language, of course, so it is up to us, as caregivers, to act in their best interest. I've designed these sections to be completed from a pet's point of view. Based on your pet's personality and likes/dislikes, it is time to walk a mile in their paws, fly with their wings, or swim with their fins…

Write down your pet's personality. Attach a recent photo. Name some of their favorite foods, pastimes, and the things they enjoy doing. You can update this yearly if you like. Attach another piece of paper if needed.

PROMISE 3:

MY COMFORT LEVELS

PROMISE 3:

My Comfort Levels

To my pet parent: I want to be treated with dignity near the end of my life. I would like to be kept comfortable. Please do your best to act on my behalf. (Cross out anything you don't agree with)

PHYSICAL

It is important to me to move about freely without pain.

It is important to me to be able to move away after urinating or defecating.

It is important to me to be able to urinate on my own.

It is important to me to be able to defecate on my own.

If I'm experiencing any sign of pain or discomfort, I would like you to help to manage it.

It is important that medication does not alter my personality.

It is important that any side effects do not outweigh the benefits.

It is important I don't get tired by walking from one part of the house to another.

It is important for me to be able to get comfortable.

APPETITE

It is important to me to be able to eat on my own.

It is important for me not to be fed by tube or forced to eat.

BEHAVIORIAL

It is important for me to have more good days than bad.

It is important for me to still want to play with you.

It is important for me not to be sad or anxious.

It is important that I am not acting distant, restless or agitated.

It is important for me to still want to initiate contact with you.

It is important for me to not be a burden to you or anyone in the family

PROMISE 4:

MY LAST WISHES

PROMISE 4:

My Last Wishes

To my pet parent: I know you would do anything in the world for me. I would like you to not prolong treatment if I have a serious chronic illness or I am so sick that I might die soon. Please do your best to act on my behalf. (Cross out anything you don't agree with)

If I have a serious chronic illness, you will work closely with a trusted veterinarian/professional for my best care.

If I have a serious chronic illness, it is okay to get a second opinion.

If I have a serious chronic illness, treatments can be tried to see if they will help.

If I have a serious chronic illness, it is okay to research online before committing to serious treatments.

If the treatments do not work and there is little hope that I will get better, I do not want prolonged things, such as radiation or chemotherapy.

It is okay to give me long-term treatments, such as chemotherapy or radiation
It is okay to explore alternative non-invasive holistic therapies.

It is okay to put me through surgery to attempt to save my life.

It is okay to put me through surgery that is not required to save my life, but may improve my medical condition.

Reminder:

Our animal friends suffer the same kind of ailments do, but because their high threshold for pain, they sometimes have a hard time letting us know they are hurting. Non-invasive, holistic practices such as veterinary chiropractic, reiki energy medicine, and acupuncture may help.

PROMISE 5:

MY AFTERCARE PLAN

PROMISE 5:

My Aftercare Plan

To my pet parent: I know this is hard to think of this right now. Think of it as taking care of business, so that all your focus and attention will be on me, when the time comes.

Just as we create end of life plans for humans, it can be helpful for us to learn about the various options available in the event of our pets' impending death. Below is a list of some of the things you might consider researching as your pet approaches senior age. (Cross out anything you don't agree with)

Euthanasia at veterinary practice
Euthanasia at home
Casket
Transport and delivery options
Cremation
  Communal: pets are placed side by side and cremated together
  Individual: pets are placed in individual compartments to insure the integrity of their remains
  Private: the pet is cremated by itself with viewing options of pet's ashes available
Funeral or memorial service
Keepsake memorial or jewelry
Pet loss support

PROMISE 5 ACTIVITY:

Write down any other wishes you have for your pet. For example, if your pet is very sociable, he might prefer a wake or life celebration party in honor of the love they brought to many. You may also wish to designate a pet charity to receive a memorial contributions.

Signing Your Promise to Me

Please make sure you sign this form in the presence of two witnesses.

I,____, ask that my veterinarian, family and care providers follow my pet's wishes as communicated and expressed in this document. This form becomes valid when my pet is unable to care for him/herself.

Signature: ____

Witnesses

Printed name of witness #1

Signature:

Phone:

Printed name of witness #2

Signature:

Phone:

This page is for additional notes

This page is for additional notes